WHAT IF

NO ONE

BELIEVED?

BY DAVID EDSALL

AN OLD LINE PUBLISHING BOOK

Printed in the United States of America

ISBN-13: 978-0-9844768-6-2

ISBN-10: 0-9844768-6-5

Looking for a publisher?

At Old Line Publishing we are always looking for authors with original manuscripts. We hope that you will contact us and share your thoughts, ideas, stories, and/or already written material with us so that we can help you turn your idea into a timeless treasure and share it with the world.

Old Line Publishing, LLC
P.O. Box 624
Hampstead, MD 21074
Toll-Free Phone: 1-877-866-8820
Toll-Free Fax: 1-877-778-3756
Email: oldlinepublishing@comcast.net
Website: www.oldlinepublishingllc.com

Dedication

The effort for this book was inspired by Pastor Lewis Groce, who showed me a journey and helped me find mine. It is dedicated to my family who shaped my faith by their actions. A special thanks to my Mom who made sure I received the Bibles belonging to my Uncle Mel and my Grandmother, of which I continue to treasure reading, and to my Uncle Ralph for telling me it will be OK.

Table of Contents

Forward

You could call this little book, Grace in a Nutshell. More specifically, it is the Theology of Grace as seen through the witness of my dear friend, David Edsall. The foundations of his witness are deeply rooted in the Lutheran concepts of Law and Gospel that he has known since childhood. But what makes this testimony special is that it is highlighted by his unique and colorful personality and perspective (which includes his love of golf). I have known Dave for many years. I know him to be a man of deeply passionate faith. His is a faith that encourages him when times are good and supports him when they are not. We have shared a friendship as each of our lives has passed through both of those extremes.

What I especially like about Dave's writing is his use of the Bible stories that when heard over and over can remain as dry words on a page. But Dave puts himself and the reader into the story and animates it with emotion. Granted they are his emotions because it would be impossible to really know what these characters were feeling. None-the-less, when you begin to see the characters as people with feelings, you can relate to them and the situation becomes real. The lesson is easier to understand.

The Grace of God is a mystery that man can only try to understand by analogy. It is similar to this example or that example but in total is always more that any one example can demonstrate. We learn about Grace through God's self-revelation in Jesus Christ as witnessed in Holy Scripture. And, we learn about it in the powerful witness of those who love Him, like Dave. Much has been written about Grace, but it is usually approached in a dry propositional form. Dave makes it personal. Dave makes it real.

Ken Holder, MD

Preface

With God All Things Are Possible

I imagine a rather cold and dreary day. Certainly not the typical sun shining spring afternoon associated with April. There was no color, just emotionless grey. A man in his mid-thirties was being sentenced and put to death by the most deplorable method known to man. Pilate tried to excuse his behavior, but the angry crowd refused to relent. This man clearly didn't deserve to die, but Pilate was eager to diffuse the inevitable ensuing riot. Finally he conceived a way out. Offer the Crowd a choice. The man he couldn't pin a crime on, or the known criminal. The Crowd made its choice.

As the crowd roared its approval, Pilate laid down the decree. Death by The Cross. No stay of execution. No waiting around on death row. Immediate. Take him away now. Through the crowded streets, the man picked up his cross and dragged his way to the top of The Hill.

A funny thing was happening along the way. As he got closer to his destination, the jeers slowed as well. Faces changed. The once angry, boisterous crowd began to wear solemn expressions. As he hung on The Cross and the sky filled with darkness, one soldier even professed, "Surely this was the Son of God."

I am sure we all have our images and depiction of That Day. God sent His Son to save the world. The world rejected Him. We don't have to go far to see people's impressions of That Day. Movies about the life of Jesus are plentiful, each with a pronounced death sequence. Some of my impressions would include a heavy sky, clouds bulging and barely hanging, portraying the mighty injustice of the day. The air was still, except for an occasional blustery gust that served to accent the level of the crowd now and then. When "It is finished," the sky grew black and buckets of cold rain covered the land. You know that rain, the kind that penetrates your skin. The kind that no matter what you do, you can't get warm.

With Jesus' death, God reconciled mankind to Himself. The Sin that had no abandon on earth, no longer held its grip on the relationship between God and man. Jesus took the Wrath of God upon His own shoulders and bore the penalty for mankind. God did what man could never do. God's Riches At Christ's Expense. GRACE.

People often ask, "What do we have to do to get God's Grace?" Gee, we killed his Son, isn't that enough? A good friend of mine who's previous work, *Fear Not* inspired this work, Lewis A. Groce, says for a lot of humans, God simply giving unconditional forgiveness is not enough. Humans have to feel important and must infuse themselves into the equation here. I must have some control over my own destiny. I need to do something. I am too important for me to just stand here and be forgiven. No such thing as a free lunch. You don't get something for nothing. If it sounds too good to be true...Some Bible "scholars" plunge into Scriptures finding ways in which man can participate in God's free outpouring of Grace. More importantly, perhaps, they can point to scripture and say "See, it says so right here." Most important of all, they say, you must believe. If you don't' believe in Jesus, His actions mean nothing to you. His death and resurrection alone don't save you, because you don't believe in Him. Oh sure, He still loves you and all. But if you don't swallow the story, you cannot be saved.

There are many religions that exist in today's ME world. Christianity, while popular to say the least, doesn't even come close to a majority in the polls. Even The Beatles were more popular than Christ. While history explains that there is more written about Jesus than any other man, it would be safe to say there is more disdain towards Christ than full, loving belief in His mission. It is written that even Jesus' own family wasn't sure what He was all about. The vast majority of people inhabiting the surrounding areas at the time Christ was on earth did not believe in His mission. They killed Him, remember? If The Crowd was even half and half, I wonder if

Pilate would have changed his mind about the conviction. But it wasn't close. Barabbas' campaign managers did a wonderful job. Jesus just wasn't popular enough.

Still, Jesus fulfilled His Mission. He went through with it. He died on The Cross to save the very people who nailed the spikes. The very people who called "Barabbas!" when the time came to choose. The very person who washed his hands with the situation. When it came right down to it, Peter, The Rock, The Stone on which the Church will stand, yes THAT Peter, HE couldn't bring himself to say he believed in Christ. Jesus' chilling proclamation came true. "Before the cock crows, three times you will deny Me." Jesus was right.

He also pleaded, "Forgive them Father, for they know not what they do." I believe Jesus in this instance as well.

Humanity, in its imperfection, can profess to believe in Christ. Still we stumble along, being human, which by nature, makes us sinful. We fall short, counting on God's Grace each and every day. For some, this free gift is recognized and realized now. God forgives, so we can go forward, being humans, falling short, by nature sinful. But God loves us first, and that gives us the lifeblood to allow us to continue on our daily dealings. For others, God's Grace doesn't quite finish the job. WE need to have some input. WE need to be doing something. God expects us to do something. Yes, the gift is free, but there has got to be some fine print somewhere.

Jesus says, "God's Grace is sufficient." Some point out that Jesus also said, "...whomever believes is me shall be saved." But what if no one believed?

Chapter One
Mulligans

Back at the church I attended in Texas, I know a couple that considered themselves Christians, and I would imagine Bible scholars. I know that is very lofty, but they did have a very vast knowledge of the Bible. They confessed to be Lutherans, speaking freely of the welcoming Martin Luther's theology of the Salvation through Grace, not through works righteous. As I became more and more enthralled in theology and more specifically, Luther's theology, I grew towards a more intentional study of the Bible. The farther along I got, the more intense the Words became. I began to look at Christ's teaching, the New Testament and the ways and means of Christ's Salvation. This, as you can imagine, led to various pointed discussions of theology and further Bible Study. I met a man at a retreat held in Lutherville, Texas. It was a Via de Cristo (Way of Christ) gathering that proved to strengthen my relationship with Christ, and got me energized into theology. The couple at my local church was instrumental in leading me to attend. This interesting man I met there was a Pastor and gave a talk about Grace that I never heard before. He talked about Grace as a mulligan from God. Now for all you non-golfers, a mulligan makes reference to a shot you make in golf that is so terrible your fellow golfers even agree that, in fact, that shot not only didn't count, but doesn't exist at all. Therefore you are allowed to hit another one. This man, Lewis A. Groce, described God's Grace as a mulligan, in fact, a perpetual mulligan. We fail miserably and God says "Go ahead, try it again. That one doesn't count." The good Reverend even went as far as to say God replaces your ball and tee, and tells you "Take another shot at it. That one doesn't count."

As you can imagine, that type of "theology" was very fresh for me. I had just begun life as a self employed golf course architect, so the golf analogy intrigued me. I made it a point to corral Lewis that weekend and we became fast friends. Lewis shared his book *Fear Not!* with me and I took it to heart. In his book, Lewis confirms what Luther was trying to establish with attempted reformation of the Catholic Church. God acts alone when it comes to salvation. Salvation is God's unconditional gift to humanity. We can attempt to please God, to do His will, to be "good," but in the long run, man cannot, will not, does not change the fact. It is the central theme throughout the Old and New Testaments. God creates and man screws it up. God creates again and the cycle continues. God Tees up a ball, man shanks one off to the left, God tees up another. Man does not deserve the mulligan. Quite frankly, as we all see later, man NEEDS the mulligan...

The couple I spoke of at the beginning of this chapter is fairly typical. They rant and rave of God's Grace, tell of the unconditional love and undying Grace God so freely gives. God gave His Son, Jesus, as a sign of His love and salvific ways. Man can do nothing, and does not deserve the "free" gift of salvation. God chooses to make this happen, and conveys His salvation through the death and resurrection of His Son, Jesus Christ. At this point, everything is just fine. However, in order to receive this free gift, the couple will contend that one must accept the gift. The acceptance takes on several forms. Belief in Christ, obedience to God's laws, and being one of the "chosen" ones are pre-requisites to your reception of God's Grace. In some of our conversations, it was intimated that you could "believe" in Christ, but lose favor with God (losing your salvation in the process) if you lived a life that conflicted with God's Will for you. Or at least their interpretation of His Will for you.

As you might imagine, several heated discussions ensued over a few years. I wouldn't say we argued, because "differences of opinion" sounds so much more poetic. We had many "differences of opinion." Why, you might ask? I believe in what Luther was trying to do in his reformation. God saves people. People do not save people. We can confess, say

"Hail Mary's" till the cows come home, beg, plead, make excuses, try "real hard" to live a "godly" life (life according to God's laws) but we will never be able to save ourselves. Or even aid in saving ourselves. God acts because only God can. In Matthew, Jesus tells us "With man this is impossible, but with God all things are possible" (20:26). This is a critical passage because Jesus told this to His disciples in answer to the question "Who then, can be saved?" Hmmm. With man this is impossible. But with God all things are possible. The exact same scenario appears in Mark (10:27). We will delve into these instances in a future chapter. The very fact that Jesus appears on earth, has a mission to do, and completes His mission, is testimony alone to Gods' reconciliation of man unto Himself. Only He can accomplish this.

But a good study of the teaching and thinking's of Martin Luther must begin in the logical place...the beginning....

Chapter Two
The Beginning

For Martin Luther, the Book of Romans was the spark he needed. Romans was written as a letter from the Apostle Paul to the Church of Rome, hence the name Romans. The church was predominately Gentile, but most likely had a fairly large spattering of Jews as well. Historians will tell you the theme of the letter is the basic Gospel, God's plan of salvation and righteousness for all mankind, Gentile and Jew alike. For Luther, it was an eye opener. Romans reeks of God's Grace.

Some historical theologians say Paul's letter reads more like an elaborate theological essay than a letter. It has twists and turns, statements, explanations, corrections and conclusions. I find the most illuminating verse in Romans is Chapter 5. Yes, the whole chapter. In it, Paul makes the timeless and irrefutable conclusion that Sin appears to the world through one man and is reconciled by one man.

> *"Consequently, just as the result of one trespass was condemnation for men, so also the result of one act of righteousness was justification that brings life for all men. For just as through the disobedience of the one man the many were made sinners, so also through the obedience of the one man the many will be made righteous."*
>
> Romans 5:18-22

In this one sequence of words, Paul ties up the theme. The one trespass, Adam's utter disobedience to God, was the undoing of man. This one act alone caused separation of mankind and God. Mankind was to reflect that disobedience to God from that moment on, unable to bridge that separation that he created. Paul recognized this simple truth. Man was forever going to represent Sin in the eyes of God. One act of man. Condemnation for mankind.

I have a feeling this effected Luther as he attempted to digest this. Man created the separation with this disobedience to God. God gave man free reign and man hit one off the tee and into the woods. (Sorry, another golf injection.) This is to say God created man and said this is good. Man turned the good creation into disobedience and sin. Man became Sin, sinful by nature. Mankind would be separate from God. Man disobeyed a direct command from God, and therefore became sinful in God's eyes. Paul equates Adam's transgression with man's downfall and assigns man's separation with God solely on this one act of disobedience. "The result of the one trespass was the condemnation of men."

Paul then observed that the act of one righteousness creates the justification of men. In the same manner as condemnation came to man because of Adam's disobedience, justification comes to man through the righteousness of one man, namely Jesus. In The Old Testament, God outlines the laws of the land. Several times. These are the Laws to live by, or so it was thought at the time (and for much of the time afterward). Religious leaders of the day (and today) embraced these Laws as salvific. There is that term again. Salvific. Having to do with our Salvation. Follow these simple (?) rules and you gain eternal life. Be good and obey. The problem with that theology is The New Testament. Yes, The New Testament.

In God's New Promise, Deal, Covenant, Testament, He tells us those rules were meant to show our transgressions. Without the Law there is no Sin, even though Sin existed before the Law, (another of Paul's interjections from Romans.) Jesus begins His ministry by announcing that He came to fulfill the Law. He knows God's plan and that the Law was meant to show our transgressions. To point out what Sin is and how it has infected our daily lives, in fact our very being. God takes matters into His own hands. He sends

Jesus to fulfill the law. The Law is much too heavy to be taken on by mere humans. They (we) ARE SIN. We are the reasons for the long list that makes up The Law in the first place. WE need to be saved from our own separation from God.

At our gatherings in Lutherhill, Texas, the site for our Via de Cristo retreats twice a year, Grace is the general theme being presented. Several pastors have presented various talks on the subject. The laypeople that give talks usually deal with more of the community and environment and today's applications. The pastors get to delve into Grace. A great example of the mixture of the two was a presentation of Lewis' conversation about the Golfing God. Mulligans! How nice! Wasn't it Lee Trevino who once said, "Even God couldn't hit a one iron"? Maybe He took a mulligan. Anyway, the Grace talks usually centered on the New Testament (NT), which was no surprise to me. Someone asked me once whether I thought God was destructive. Hmmm. I never really gave that much thought. She told me all I had to do was simply read the Old Testament... I never really gave the OT much reading time. I was stuck in the NT, especially after all this Grace talk. Pastor Jesse Essinger, a long standing VdC'er gave a Grace talk that centered on God's Grace. Except he was stuck in the OT. "No more enthralling," said Jesse, "is God's Grace so abundantly expressed than in the OT." Hmmm, again. Gee I think I should read some of that stuff. So I did. Jesse was right. The good ole OT depicts a gracious God who time and time again teed the ball back up for mankind. My guess is I was sleeping all through Sunday School. If you ever need some examples of down and out circumstances that faced people early on, read the OT. You get some clues about what was in store for the future of mankind as well. Aside from being very prophetic about the ensuing NT, the OT is wonderfully littered with great stories of God's Grace. Jesse likes to point out that even life itself is testament to God's Grace. The daily breath we take is God's gift....

"He went to Nazareth, where he had been brought up, and on the Sabbath Day he went into the synagogue, as was his custom. And he stood up to read. The scroll of the prophet Isaiah was handed to him. Unrolling it, he found the place where it was written: 'The Spirit of the Lord is in me, because it has anointed me to preach the good news to the poor. He has sent me to proclaim freedom to the prisoners, and recovery of sight for the blind, to release the oppressed, to proclaim the year of the Lord's favor.' Then he rolled up the scroll, gave it back to the attendant, and sat down. The eyes of everyone in the synagogue were fastened on him, and he began by saying to them, 'Today this scripture is fulfilled in your hearing.'"

Luke 4:14-21

A little history about the passage Jesus read is in order. "The year of the Lord's Favor" is a reference to a period when salvation would be proclaimed. This proclamation from Isaiah refers back to Leviticus 25, The Year of Jubilee, when every 50 years slaves were freed, debts were cancelled and property was returned to original family. Of course, reading this passage in present day (Jesus time) held a much more significant meaning. "He sent me to proclaim freedom to the prisoners..." Jesus knows the elders of the community would know the significance of the reading and more importantly, His proclamation that "Today this scripture is fulfilled in your hearing."

Jesus used this opportunity to pronounce His purpose. Freedom for the prisoners. More accurately, God's salvation for mankind. I believe Jesus uses this passage because He knows the "religious right" would understand perfectly what He was referring to. The parallels are too significant to ignore. Freedom for the prisoners. Not because they deserved it. Not because of good actions. Not even because they had turned from their ways that caused their imprisonment in the first place. Just as the original OT passage granted mercy upon the imprisoned, so does Jesus' proclamation of fulfillment. Merciful granting of pardon. Wrongs righted. Gracious forgiving of debts. In short, the Gospel Message in a nutshell.

It is clear to me the congregation gathered at the synagogue that day understood exactly what Jesus said and what He meant. Their reaction? Disbelief in His words and angry resentment. The Bible even says they drove Him out and were prepared to stone Him right there. But Jesus just walked through the crowd and went His way, untouched. The rejection of His mission had only just begun there. Jesus spent His entire days on earth in rejection of His Word. Sure He had followers, groves of them. They listened intently to His sermons, questioned Him continuously, and even tested.

Did anyone in His time, I mean the ones who were actually there with Him as he walked the earth, did any of these fellow members of mankind really believe in Him? I mentioned our most fallible Peter previously. Peter is often talked about in the pastoral circles as the most "human" of the disciples. I can hear Jesus giving the eulogy at Peter's funeral, using the famous words of Captain James T. Kirk, USS Enterprise (Star Trek fame) when he gave homage to a fallen comrade, namely Spock, by saying "…in all my travels, his soul was the most…human."

Peter had a knack of declaring the obvious without really knowing what he was saying. Jesus asked his disciples who the people said He was. Some said Elijah reborn; some said John the Baptist reincarnated. "But who do you say I am?" Jesus asked. Peter blurted out "You are the Son of God, the Messiah." Jesus was pleased with his disciple. He began to tell them what was about to happen to Him. Peter attempted to "save" Him from what was to happen. In one discussion, Peter went from hero to goat. "Get thee behind me Satan." Huh? Peter must have done a double take. He didn't understand. "You are the Christ, the Son of the Living God."

He didn't comprehend Jesus' mission, or rather how it was to be fulfilled. Peter demonstrates fear for Jesus' safety here, I think. Could he say that Jesus was the Son of God and still be concerned about things to come without some measure of disbelief?

We see Peter's less than 100% commitment to the overall picture again in another instance. Jesus came to the disciples as they lay in their boat on the water. Peter sees Jesus walking on the water towards them. Jesus holds out His hand and for a moment, Peter is fine. Then his humanism takes over and he has a blip of disbelief. Peter, after all, was human…

Chapter Three
I Am The Way

"The teachers of the Law and the Pharisees brought in a woman caught in adultery. They made her stand before the group and said to Jesus, 'Teacher, this woman was caught in the act of adultery. In the Law Moses commanded us to stone such a woman. Now what do you say?' They were using this question as a trap, in order to have a basis to accuse him. But Jesus bent down and started to write on the ground with his finger. When they kept questioning him, he straightened up and said to them, "if any one of you is without sin, let him throw a stone at her.' Again he stooped down and wrote on the

ground. At this, those who heard began to go away one at a time, the older ones first until Jesus was the only one left. Jesus straightened up and asked her, 'Woman, where are they? Has no one condemned you?' 'No one sir,' she said. 'Then neither do I condemn you,' Jesus declared, 'Go now and leave your life of sin.'"

John 8:3-11

This is one of my favorite verses in John. The "religious right" of the day seemingly had Jesus this time. If He let this woman go, He would be denouncing the Law of Moses. If He allowed her to be stoned to death, which the Law commanded them to do, what would that say about His teaching on forgiveness and love? The congregants were looking, hoping for a mistake by Jesus. Something they could take back to their leaders and accuse Him.

But Jesus doesn't let that happen. Not yet anyway. He really doesn't even answer their question. Rarely when someone answers a question with a question, does the original question get answered. Jesus turns the tables on their consciences. He allows them to answer their own question in their own manner. "If anyone among you is without sin, let him cast the first stone." There could only be one answer to that question. Of course the only one without sin is the one who is left with the woman. Yet this one doesn't cast a stone. Instead he declares non-condemnation. This gets overlooked sometimes. Jesus was left with the woman. According to His own response, "If any is without sin..." Jesus is without sin. "...he can cast the first stone." This was well within Jesus' right, according to the Law. But as we discussed earlier, Jesus was to fulfill the Law. He would take on the penalty for Sin.

I have heard many sermons using this passage as the base. Usually you will hear about how Jesus uses this particular circumstance to show how we should not stand in judgment of each other, especially when we have our own transgressions to consider. How could one who sins condemn another sinner? Of course the crowd knows that the Roman law did not allow them to carry out their own death sentences (which led to Pilate becoming involved in Jesus' execution.) So, if Jesus had said to stone her according to the Law of Moses, he could be persecuted according to Roman law. If He said not to stone her, He would invalidate their own law. But Jesus let them carry out the sentence with a new twist. Let the non-sinner decide. Which is exactly what happened.

Others preach that the verses here describe Jesus' love and compassion. He certainly had that. "...nor do I condemn you." The woman had been caught red handed. No one stood for her defense, because there was none. She was guilty. But Jesus showed her compassion. She was free to go.

This passage has so much more to offer, and its implication is much broader. What we see happening here is extremely illuminating. Jesus offers a taste of why He came to earth to begin with. With His words and deeds in this instance, Jesus showcases His mission. "With man, this is impossible, but with God all things are possible." Remember that one? Here is the application of those words.

Jesus says here that He offers no condemnation. Now there is no denying guilt. As a matter of fact, Jesus doesn't even address the transgression. Guilt is unquestioned. I believe this symbolizes that sin is sin, and there is no distinction between transgressions. There are no levels of sin. There isn't a list of "bad sins," "really bad sins" and "unforgivable sins." The transgression doesn't really come into play. The fact of the matter is sin itself. As we learned in Romans, sin originates with Adam. Humanity itself represents sin. Sinful by nature. We say that every week in our Creed. "We are by nature sinful and unclean." It is interesting that anyone in the crowd that brought the woman before Jesus could have been in place of the woman. Any one of them could have been on trial, for of course they all had sinned. And this leads to their disbursement.

"Nor do I condemn you." Jesus says His mission is not of condemnation, but of salvation. John 3:17 "For God did not send His Son into the world to condemn the world, but to save the world through Him." Jesus tells this woman He does not condemn her for her actions, her sinful actions. The woman does not confess her belief to Jesus. The Bible gives no indication that this woman knows Jesus at all. She offers no repentance, nor does she offer any defense. Just guilt.

She represents the sin she is accused of and stands at the door of mercy.

It is fairly clear that Jesus knows of her guilt as well. Aside from the fact that God knows all, in the Jewish community, to accuse someone of breaking a law, circumstantial evidence is not allowed. Only firsthand witness was proper evidence. Yes it was perfectly clear that this woman was guilty. "Teacher, this woman was caught in the act of adultery."

Once Jesus clears the area free of the humanistic thought process of condemnation, He grants this testimony to sin forgiveness. No condemnation. Not as a response to her faith. Not because she pleads for mercy, repents or shows any sorrow. Just pure mercy, poured out by Jesus. An indication of His mission. Salvation. Freedom for the prisoners. Undeserving, yet unconditional.

One of the most recited verses of the Bible is, of course, John 3:16. Recall all those sporting events with the guy with multicolored hair, holding the sign in the end zone, behind the basket, in centerfield, wherever a camera can see him? We see this board flash in movies, commercials, parades, stock car races et al. Once more, for the record.

"For God so loved the world that he gave his one and only Son, that whoever believes in him shall not perish but have eternal life."

John 3:16

For the record, once again, let's recite the entire passage, which actually begins at the beginning of the chapter. Thus, read.

> "Now there was a man of the Pharisees name Nicodemus, a man of the Jewish ruling council. He came to Jesus at night and said 'Rabbi, we know you are a teacher who comes from God. For no one could perform the miraculous signs you are doing if God were not with him.' In his reply, Jesus declared, 'I tell you the truth; no one can see the kingdom of God unless he is born again.' 'How can a man be born when he is old?' Nicodemus asked. 'Surely he cannot enter a second time into his mother's womb to be born!' Jesus answered, 'I tell you the truth; no one can enter the kingdom of God unless he is born of water and the Spirit. Flesh gives birth to flesh, but the Spirit gives birth to spirit. You should not be surprised by my saying 'You must be born again.' The wind blows wherever it pleases. You hear its sound but you cannot tell where it comes from or where it is going. So it is with everyone born of the Spirit.' 'How can this be?' Nicodemus asked. 'You are Israel's teacher,' said Jesus, 'and you do not understand these things? I tell you the truth, we speak of what we know, and testify to what

we have seen, but still you people do not accept our testimony. I have spoken to you of earthly things and you do not believe. How then will you believe if I speak of heavenly things? No one has ever gone into heaven except the one who came from heaven – the Son of Man. Just as Moses lifted up the snake in the desert, so the Son of Man must be lifted up, that everyone who believes in him may have eternal life. For God so loved the world that he gave his one and only Son, that whoever believes in him shall not perish but have eternal life. For God did not come into the world to condemn the world, but to save the world through him. Whoever believes in him is not condemned, but whoever does not believe in him stands condemned already because he has not believed in the name of God's one and only Son. This is the verdict: Light has come into the world, but men loved darkness instead of the light because their deeds were evil. Everyone who does evil hates the light, and will not come into the light for fear that his deeds will be exposed. But whoever lives by the truth comes into the light so that it may be seen plainly that what he has done has been done through God.'"

John 3: 1-21

Jesus explains this to a confused Nicodemus. Note the scripture says Nicodemus came to Jesus at night. That is interesting in itself. But Nicodemus doesn't really ask Jesus anything, he just describes, even adulates Jesus as a special messenger from God. Jesus rebukes him, well sort of. He tells Nicodemus something that, of course, Nicodemus does not comprehend, or expect, I would gather. Be born again? What gives here, Jesus? How can that be? Then Jesus gets to the heart of His message to Nicodemus.

Nicodemus, described here by Jesus as Israel's teacher. Israel, the keeper of the Law. A member of the Pharisees, the Jewish law keepers. It is unclear what reason Nicodemus had for even seeking Jesus out that night. In his conversation this night with Jesus, he learns much more about the mission for which he could have bargained. Jesus tells him that He is the way, the truth and the light. Jesus even tells Thomas this later in John. Having this as a forerunner to John 3:1-21, we can dissect His words to gather meaning.

I believe the Bible represents a Living Word. Everyone who reads the Bible will gather meaning and illumination, because the Bible speaks to the heart. Everyone's heart is different and the Words will have meaning unto themselves in your heart. The best evidence we have to this is the many religions we have in the world, and the many disagreements that stem from interpretation. A good friend of mine, and a wonderful man, Pastor Fred Toerne, once told me that as many people that have, are and will walk the face of the earth, that is how many ways there are to Christ. How true!

God encompasses all beliefs, religions, hearts and spirit. We are many, but we are all one body in Christ.

Jesus describes Himself as the Light. "Light has come into the world..." the meaning, the Truth, yes Light itself. Mankind has been shrouded in darkness since the "fall from God," now gets to bask in the Light. Jesus, God, has come into the world to reveal the true nature of Himself. Sometimes we hear people talk about the "fall from Grace." Darkness, separation from God, SIN, running rampant, in fact, falling "into" Grace. Without our transgressions, what is the necessity for Grace at all? But alas, we are humans. However, that is a different topic and we will delve into that later...

Jesus describes Himself as the Light. "Light has come into the world..." The Truth is now revealed in the Word. In John, Chapter One, we learn that in the beginning was The Word and The Word was with God and The Word was God. Then The Word becomes Flesh. Becomes Flesh. Living amongst us. In another word, Human, God, The Word, becomes Human. This human represents God. In Jesus' self description, He is The Word, The Truth and the Life. He also says "I am the Light of the world." Light has come into the world. The Truth revealed.

"Light has come into the world..." the true nature of God. This has always baffled me. Can't God "fix" things without sacrificing Jesus? Yes, mankind is SIN, all the way back to Adam. Can't God say, "Look, you people screwed up, but I forgive you...AGAIN." Well He does but in the instance of sending Jesus here to earth. We will look at this in another chapter.

God reconciles mankind to Himself, as He lays the blame for sinful natured humans on the shoulders of the only one who can handle the situation. But that is just a fraction of what is going on here. Jesus' LIFE holds significant clues to our life. Re-read the John passage again. Read what it tells us about Jesus' mission.

"Light has come into the world, but men loved darkness instead of the light because their deeds were evil. Everyone who does evil hates the light, and will not come into the light for fear that his deeds will be exposed. But whoever lives by the truth comes into the light so that it may be seen plainly that what he has done has been done through God."

Basically, Jesus is saying here that man loves the darkness because there he isn't "exposed" for his own deeds. Everyone who does evil (mankind's sinful nature) will not come into the light (Jesus) for fear...Fear. Mankind lives a fearful life because mankind represents sin in the eyes of God. The Catholics tend to emphasize this dramatically. You are sin. You must confess and pay the price. If there were "good" men, according to the Catholics, there would be no need for confession at all. And, no need for "payment" for your deeds. Ask your Catholic buddies if such a "man" exists…

"But whoever lives by the truth"…now who can live by the truth? A non sinner? We all are guilty of sin, and by definition, in conflict with the truth, for in order to live by the truth, we mustn't sin. Now we know we are sinful by nature. Whoever lives by the truth (and there can be only one) comes into the light (Jesus appearance on earth) so that it may be seen plainly that what he has done has been done through God. Jesus' life on earth was lived "in the light." In fact, He IS the light. He is the Truth. Truth living in the Light. So that it may be plainly seen that what he has done has been done through God.

Now Jesus says in the famous and repeated verses in John, that the Son of Man has come, not to condemn the world, but to save it. To reveal God's Grace and mercy. To fulfill the Law. In a discussion at our church, a question arose regarding the very story we covered about casting the first stone. Wasn't Jesus calling for a new attitude here? One person argued that Jesus did not come here to "change" the Law. She argued Jesus' mission was not to excuse the laws, making it less uncomfortable for humans to break the laws. The discussion at church actually involved a heated parlay involving homosexuality. The person argues that Jesus mission was not about making people comfortable. She was correct, but for the very reason she was arguing against. Jesus came to make DRASTIC changes in our thinking and our response to The Law. His appearance on Earth was to make wholesale changes. He changed EVERYTHING. Jesus gives humans a new commandment: "To love one another as yourself, even as I have loved you." He didn't come to change the Law; He came to fulfill the Law. He came to change our hearts. He came to show humans how to love, live and share in the Grace God gives. The Law was given to show us what our transgressions are. Jesus says, "I came to give life, and to give it abundantly." He doesn't speak about what WE can do to change OUR hearts. Jesus comes to give us the means to live. He comes to say even though you represent sin, God, in His mercy, sends me in your place to redeem you to Him. I do this, not because you deserve, warrant, or even ask me to. This is God's wish. This is God's Way.

Jesus says, "I am The Way..." So what does all this have to do with believing in Jesus? Let's take a look...

Chapter Four
Prodigal Sons
(and Daughters, too)

Now Thomas (called Didymus) one of the Twelve, was not with the disciples when Jesus came. So the other disciples told him, "We have seen the Lord!'"

But he said to them, "Unless I see the nail marks in his hands and put my finger where the nails were, and put my hand into my side, I will not believe it." A week later his disciples were in the house again and Thomas was with them. Though the doors were locked, Jesus came and stood among them, and said "Peace be with you!" Then he said to Thomas, "Put your finger here; see my hands. Reach your hand and put it into my side. Stop doubting and believe."

Thomas said to him, "My Lord and my God!"

Then Jesus told him, "Because you have seen me, you have believed; blessed are those who have not seen and yet have believed."

Jesus did many other miraculous signs in the presence of his disciples, which are not recorded in this book. But these are written that you may believe that Jesus is the Christ, the Son of God, and that by believing you may have life in his name.

John 20:24-31

Doubting Thomas. Pastor Fred Toerne always says Thomas gets a bad rap. He likes to express "doubting Thomas" as "Believing Thomas." For in the end, when presented with Jesus' presence, he of course pronounced "My Lord and my God!" Pastor Fred always points out that Thomas never does feel the nail holes, or puts his hand into Jesus' side. Thomas didn't need any other reassurance. Still he makes the proclamation.

John talks about believing as a means to life. Jesus says He is the life. The Way. Jesus says in John 14:6 "I am the way, the truth and the life." And in John 10:10 "I came that they may have life, and to have it to the full." Throughout the passages and quotations attributed to Jesus, He constantly talks about giving life. He says there are things only He can do, but believing in Him grants life. Jesus is pretty clear about His mission, and I believe His mission has many meanings.

Matthew 6:34 "Therefore do not worry about tomorrow, for tomorrow will worry about itself. Each day has enough trouble of its own." Jesus is speaking about worry and its destructive attributes. He says God will take care of us. God grants life through Jesus.

Let's go back to the passage concerning Nicodemus. Jesus declares no man can have life (or come to the Father) without being "reborn." He also tells Nicodemus that this is impossible with man. Mankind gets "reborn" through life, death and resurrection of Jesus Christ. We are Sin. Jesus grants reconciliation to God. Rebirth. A new beginning. A new Covenant, a New Testament. Not through actions by man, this is impossible. Only God can bridge the separation. With Christ's actions, God takes care or our "tomorrow." No need to worry about that. Let us worry about what unfolds today. Jesus tells us not to be paralyzed by thoughts of our unworthiness. We are reborn with His resurrection, His mission. Made right by the act of the one man who can give us rebirth.

But Jesus' mission doesn't end on that note. Jesus gives us the keys to LIFE in addition to claiming victory over death. "I came to give life..." Follow me and life abounds. Jesus spends so much time and effort on how to live now that we are freed from the "bondage of sin." Notice Jesus doesn't abolish sin, but the "bondage of sin." He serves our sentence and pays our penance. Now that the penalty has been paid, we are free from the worry of being acceptable to God, because of Jesus. So Jesus gives us the recipe for living. Not with fear of being the sinful beings that we are, that hasn't changed. Living with the blessings of the Father, living according to the truth.

The book of Matthew gives us the Beatitudes (Chapters 5-7). It is worth studying. I will allow this time for you to get your New Testament out and read these...

"Blessed are..." Jesus says, "Blessed are...the poor in spirit..." "The meek..." "The unworthy..." What I don't see is "Blessed are the righteous...blessed are the law keepers... blessed are the believers..." It is clear Jesus came for the weak in spirit, the weak in flesh. Freedom for the prisoners. When He spoke of Freedom in His proclamation at that first service, the congregation was confused. Freedom? Why, we aren't slaves to anyone. We are free. What does this mean? But as we discussed earlier, I believe the religious leaders knew of Jesus' implications here.

Throughout His walk on Earth, Jesus sat, ate, congregated, slept, fed, nourished, sheltered, healed and consoled the wretched spirits that inhabited the earth. His focus was the human spirit, the very human spirit that was separated from God by the actions of Adam. Time and time again, Jesus healed. Not just in the physical sense. He healed with His words as well as his actions. Parables to give meaning to His mission. Healing words. Of course, a lot of Jesus' parables were confusing, and most of them were subject matters that people didn't want to hear about. We all have our favorite parables, the Good Samaritan, the Prodigal Son, and so on. Most of them hold different meanings depending on our foundational understandings and beliefs. I have always wondered why Jesus seemed so figurative in His answers to the apostles and people in general. A majority of the time, it seems, people walked away from Jesus scratching their heads, like Nicodemus does. Huh? What does THAT mean? Let's take a look as some of these parables.

In the Prodigal son, we see a host of things going on. We have a kingdom of sorts, a wealthy man with two kids, on a nice plantation, both of whom stand to inherit a considerable and tidy sum, not just of wealth, but property, livestock, workers, just about everything one could ask for. One day, the younger son decides this isn't all he wants. Independence, a chance to go out and see for himself what the world brings. He no longer needs his father, he is ready to go out and make a name for himself. But wait. Of course he needs a starting point. So he goes and tells his father to give him his inheritance now. I imagine with a heavy heart the loving father agrees. The young lad goes off into the sunset, with his fortune in tow.

A funny thing happened on the way to the market. While his wealth was vast, it doesn't take too long to exhaust. The young man, in his bullet-proof nature, quickly consumes his fortune. With no guidance from "Dad," and left to his own devices, the full disclosure of his money is used on lavishness, I would assume. And the Bible tells us, along with his disappearing fortune so goes his friends. Left alone, penniless, and without work, the young man starts to feel the pinch of the ensuing drought. Now, for the first time, not only does he have wants, he has needs. Finally he finds a farmer who gives him a job tending to the pigs. This is a significant point of the story because in Bible times, pigs were considered the lowest forms of life. They were dirty. They were disgusting and filthy. It is intentional that Jesus says the youngster felt envious of the pigs; at least they had something to eat. The original audience would know this man could not stoop any lower than this. Eating "food" meant for the pigs. Unthinkable.

Finally of course, the young man comes to his senses. He realizes what he really needs is his father. He was warm, never hungry, and had his wants and needs attended to when he was home. He wonders that if he begs hard enough, maybe his father will let him work on the plantation, and at least he wouldn't hunger. So, he sets off back across the countryside, with only a glimmer of hope, beating himself up with every step that takes him closer to his former home. He is trying to figure out what to say. Over and over he rehearses his lines, praying that he can find the proper words to gain his father's acceptance. At this point, he would rejoice and be glad if his father would even allow him back on the estate at all.

Off in the distance, he sees the house. He probably walks with shorter steps, unsure of how he will be received, wondering over and over again if the words he has chosen will be sufficient. I imagine he doesn't even notice, off in the distance that his father has seen him coming, and is racing around, overjoyed to see his son returning. As he nears the main house, he is greeted by a host of servants. They put a robe around his shoulders. They bring sandals for his blistered feet. Put rings on his fingers. Anoint his sun baked skin with oils. He is dazed; he doesn't understand what is happening. When he realizes that his father is quickly approaching him, he straightens his head, ready with his apologetic speech, still unsure of the reaction, but ready to face whatever consequences await him.

He lowers his head and stoops before his father. "Dad, I have been foolish. I squandered the inheritance you gave me. Your money, your wealth. Dad, I am hungry, yet I do not deserve to be your son. Let me work among the servants you have."

This is what he wants to say, and I imagine the youngster probably got most of it out. However, we know it fell on deaf ears. For the father had his own agenda. So overjoyed that his son is back, he doesn't hear the plea. He is busy lifting his son from the ground. Busy ordering the servants to see to his needs. Busy getting the feast ready. "Bring the fatted calf! We are going to have a feast," he proclaims. The young man's head is spinning. "But Dad, I am not worthy, I came to beg your mercy. I have squandered…"

Before he realizes the full weight of what has materialized, the son is sitting at the head of the table, eating food he couldn't even imagine a short time ago, drinking the finest wine. His father by his side, swelling with pride and overjoyed that his son has returned, tells him his apology is unnecessary. His love for his son never diminished.

Jesus uses this parable to illustrate our relationship with God. God gives us humans all the riches He creates. Full reign over His creation. The pot at the end of the rainbow. We couldn't have wanted any more. All our needs and wants taken care of.

But as we know, mankind squanders this relationship. He decides he doesn't need God, we can do it alone. "Father, give me my inheritance, for I am ready to go it alone." The loving Father abides the wishes. Just as the youngster in the parable, we soon find out just how fragile we are…

I believe the real focus in the parable is this…God, like the father in the parable, never lost his love for the son, humankind. The son, man, did the unspeakable, still the father, God, never leaves his son. His love is always with him. He never disowns his son.

God doesn't turn His back on man. The graceful actions God chooses to show is in spite of our actions to Him. We, even though we cause our own separation with God, can't dissolve His love for us. Our actions will never overcome God's love for us. His reconciliation, with Jesus' life, death and resurrection, clinches man's eternal fate. His love never leaves us. We do not deserve the fate God has paved for us. We deserve to be left out with the pigs; we are by nature sinful and unclean. Unclean, like the pigs. I imagine the father in the parable heard about his son's actions. Why don't you do something, I am sure he was asked often. How can you stand by and let your wealth be swept away? That son is no good. He wants to leave? He wants to wallow in lavishness?

Our lives are sometimes like that. We don't know how good we have it. Our very roots were grounded in God's paradise. Mankind hit one into the woods. God's ultimate mulligan, Jesus, came to the rescue. God knows our imperfections, our shortcomings. Yet, His love goes unchanged and undaunted. He robes us in silk, gives us the feast to end all feasts.

Back to the parable. Jesus throws in a wrinkle. The oldest son. He works all day in his father's plantation. He supervises the workers. He maintains his father's holdings. He lives under his father's roof. If you looked up the "perfect son" in the dictionary, his picture would be there. A father couldn't ask for a "better" son. I am sure dad was very proud of his oldest son.

When the youngster decided to leave, I am sure his older brother was not amused. How stupid could this kid be? He wants to leave? Surely dad isn't going to stand for this. I imagine he is stunned when his father divides his wealth and gives the younger one half. Is the old man crazy? He is just going to waste all this. You can't be serious, dad. With great compassion, dad explains to his oldest son that it will be okay. I can see the oldest son trudging back out to the fields, disgusted with his brother and shocked by his father's actions.

There exists a faction of humankind that has this behavior pattern. They look down on the "younger sons" with disgust, knowing that the "Father" isn't going to stand for the actions of those youngsters. Just like the older son, they are willing to write off the younger brother. Good riddance. We don't need you. If you want to leave, so be it. Take what you will and never come back. You are not part of the family anymore. There is even an air of not wanting to be associated with the younger son. They may hear stories of action by the younger brother. They roll their eyes in contempt. They judge and declare what a fool the younger brother has become. They may even claim no knowledge of his existence. They point to their own chests and feel redemptive because of their actions of obedience to the father. Surely the father will reward me for my actions. My time is coming because I have toiled away here on my father's estate. I will get what I deserve eventually.

Jesus returns to the older brother in the parable. He hears the rowdy crowd, not knowing what the celebration is about. He wasn't informed of any party. What is going on here? He sends a servant back to the house to see what is up. When the servant returns, the son is beside himself. WHAT? HE is back? And there is a party? Has dad lost his mind? He knows what the youngster has done. He squandered everything that was his, and it wasn't even his to begin with.

The elder son refuses to attend. He shuns the party, disgusted with his brother, his father and the entire affair. He sulks in the field, very unhappy and feeling bitter. Contempt. Why do I deserve this treatment? Haven't I been everything my father wanted me to be? Haven't I devoted my life to him? Why would he embrace that loser other son of his? What has he done to deserve these things? He wasted his inheritance. Why, why, why???

Again, Jesus uses the feeling of the oldest to depict a faction of humankind. The glass is half empty here. Why would someone get something for nothing? Why does he get the things I know I deserve to get? He hasn't done anything to warrant the Father's love. I did my father's will. I was here tending to things. I didn't go off and live the foolish life. I have been good. I deserve the things my brother is getting and more. He is getting the rewards.

When the father learns of his older son's contempt and disgust, he leaves the party to seek him out. As the father approaches the oldest son, he finds a bitter man. The eldest sees his father and turns his back, utterly appalled. The father proceeds, anxious to set his son's attitude back on track, and probably a little surprised at the elder's reaction to the events. "Son, please come join the festivities. Your brother has returned!"

The son spins around. "He is NOT my brother. Why do you treat him like this? You know the stories. He lost everything you gave him. He lost our wealth, OUR belongings! Why would you even speak to him again? Haven't you seen what I have done for you? I have never left your side. I tended the affairs here. I did not ask you for anything. I am obedient to your wishes. Why do you give to him what I should be getting?"

Does this sound familiar? It should, as it is only human nature. We should get what we deserve. Reap what we sow. Our actions will depict our rewards. But the Father has a different view…

"My son, you have been with me, and all that I own is yours. But your brother was lost and now he is found. Your brother was dead, now alive! Let us rejoice in this news! Come, join the feast!"

This is very dramatic. It is a foreshadowing of God's Grace. "God's Grace is sufficient." I saw a comic in the paper one day. It was The Family Circle, I am sure you are familiar with the daily cartoon. In this episode, the mother is busy holding the baby, who is crying. The older son is messing about, the daughter is busy with something else, everyone is screaming. Even the dog is getting into trouble. She is answering the door, and the visitor asks, "With so many kids here, how do you divide your love?" Her reply is, "You don't divide your love, you multiply it." What a beautiful way to depict God's Grace. It isn't divided among the "deserving." It is multiplied to include even the undeserving. God's Grace is sufficient.

Our reaction to people too often resembles the oldest son's. Why did he get what I so surely deserve? Jesus' parable looks at this from a different standpoint. I believe he is saying "is what you have any less because of how I multiply my Grace?" Like the father in the parable, He says, "you are with me and all I have is yours." Nothing changes that. Not mercy for another sinner. Multiplied, not divided. My Grace is sufficient for ALL. Because I choose to be merciful to your brother, does that make my Grace for you any less sufficient?

How many times have we been in this position? Someone gets passed over, or so it seems. People who you least expect to succeed, do. Maybe even at our expense, or so it seems. For many people, the glass is half empty. Not only that, but they have contempt because other people get that which they feel they deserve. The thing is, their riches are not diminished at all, but they focus on the rewards of others and have to compare deeds. The final score. Why is it so hard to swallow that God decides everyone wins?

I hear a lot of times that another facet of this story centers on how the younger son repented to get his father's love back. He (the son) made the first move toward reconciliation. He came back and the father took him in. They equate that to our relationship with God. We, by nature, are the prodigal son. When we realize our wasteful ways and decide to come back to our Father, then he will love us again, and take us in. But, we need to repent. We need to make the first step. We need to come back to the fold.

The reality of God's love never left us. Our sinful nature aside, He sent His Son to claim our future. He overcame death, which is our penance of our sins. Jesus took the keys to death and makes them His own. With the emptiness of the tomb on Easter Sunday, so is the emptiness of our penance, our separation from God. Nothing we do can change our Father's love for us. He continues to shower us in silk robes, rings and the fatted calf. Sometimes we may stray, taking our "inheritance" with us. But that doesn't change the outcome. God's love is unconditional, undying.

Sometimes we feel like the Prodigal Son, not knowing how to "get right with God." We have wandered off the path of His will, and feel like we don't deserve His love. In the words of Lewis Groce, we can "Fear Not!" Jesus tells us God's love is unswerving!! That is the Good News of the New Testament. We ARE loved and claimed by God, just as "He is RISEN!"

Chapter Five
Ways to Christ

"Of all the people that have, are, and will walk the face of the earth, that is how many different ways there are to Christ"
– Pastor Fred Toerne

Pastor Fred Toerne, a pastor I met at a Via de Cristo weekend in Lutherhill, Texas teaches about Grace. With these words, Fred speaks volumes about how Jesus comes to us. Each of us in our own way. I mentioned this phrase earlier. In my own travels through Bible study and theology, I received several Bibles, the first one I got was back in middle school days called *The Way*. It was written in the "modern" language of the day. *The Way* was supposed to target a younger audience and was a popular gift for first communion, or confirmation and I would imagine made Sunday School a little easier to teach and understand. The book was easier to read, but a lot of the translations were most likely a little less accurate. That didn't change the impact of the words. To some "scholars," *The Way* was not much more than rubbish, certainly. But I know many of the kids my age (at the time anyway) found the words illuminating. Does this type of "modernized message" lessen the meaning? I suppose it all depends on the presentation.

I was given *The Living Bible*, the green book belonging to my grandmother. Grandma passed on and I remember my mother was adamant about me getting Grandma's Bible. This was the one she joyfully read to her grandkids before bedtime and I often saw her reading it almost any time of the day. When I opened the pages, I believe there was at least as much handwritten comments in the margins as there were printed words. I can often hear my grandmother's voice as I read the passages and her commentary.

My mother also made sure I received my great Uncle Mel's black Bible. It has black electric tape along the exterior holding it together. I don't think duct tape was around back then. Again, I can remember sitting on Uncle Mel's lap, eating Aunt Sally's ice cream as Uncle Mel read. These Bibles are treasures to me, bringing back fond memories. Each is filled with notes, highlights and commentary. When I struggle to find significance to a particular verse or verses, I find myself going back to these to see what Grandma and Uncle Mel may have said. Sometimes they have different slants on the same verses.

"...that is how many different ways there are to Christ."

What does it mean to "believe in Christ?"

As I discussed earlier, I believe the Bible is a living document, and Pastor Toerne's timeless words validate this. The Bible speaks to us as individuals, to our heart and personal being. Your particular upbringing environment establishes the foundation of your belief, and the words reflect that foundation. Your own translations take on the character of the environment that is you. In this manner, God speaks to you through the timeless words of his apostles. Even the writers' had their own perspective, their own circumstance, their own environment.

When people discuss "belief" and "understanding" and "translation," it is difficult to assess exactly what that means. Does it take a Bible scholar to determine what a passage says? Surely some amount of history is involved in a translation, but what does that really show? Is that "traditional view" really relevant today?

I get involved in many discussions about "what the Bible says." There are vastly differing opinions on what The Book says, and more importantly to those who argue their own points, what it "means." Does a study of the Bible have to agree with "conventional wisdom?" It depends on the perspective. Even within denominations, congregations and even among friends, there are often wide disagreements as to meanings of passages and applications of the words. I have seen many instances of people using single quotes taken out of context that read a certain way would promote a certain principle. These quotes, when read a certain "other way" would take on the opposite meaning. This is how wars begin. The battle to be "right" or even "righteous" becomes the most important thing.

I was told in one Bible discussion that I needed to be careful about what I say because God punishes more harshly those who teach the "wrong" idea. Huh? I used the quote Martin Luther said to his detractors at the verge of the Reformation; "Here I stand, I can do no other." Each of us has that answer available to us. The Bible speaks to the heart, and your heart makes the words come alive. I take it my Grandmother found writing down her thoughts next to the printed words helped her.

Some people contend there are "basic truths" that don't require translation - if, of course, you believe the way they do. I am not quite sure exactly what those basic truths are. A lot of times, people trying to impart their "righteous" beliefs use this tool to make you see their perspective. "If we can agree on certain principles..." (then it will become easier for you to see why I am right and you are wrong - that is the usual, albeit unspoken, ending of that phrase). I don't know why it is so important for some to impart their own perspective on someone else. I guess perhaps it validates their own ideals, but again, I don't know why that is so important. Does that make it "true-er?"

People struggle over just about anything these days. A

council president in our church once joked about a particular situation which called for a vote by the congregation, and his assessment was boiled down to a brilliant observation. He said "can we get to the vote without a discussion of the color of the ballots?" Seemed funny at the time, but how true! We lose the perspective of discussion by focusing on the irrelevant.

What does this have to do with "believing?"

Jesus often asked his disciples who people said He was, and asked who THEY thought He was. Peter gave his answer – "you are the Christ, the Son of the Living God." I believe Peter was being brutally honest about his answer. He, and the gang of 12, followed Jesus closely for a number of years, hearing His words and testifying to His deeds. Surely, after giving up their own livelihoods to follow Him, they believed in Him. It would have been difficult, I think, to NOT believe in Jesus.

I discussed some of Peter's dis-belief in an earlier chapter. Peter had several instances of "wavering" support of Jesus. Even after his declaration of "you are the Christ..." Peter didn't really understand, or perhaps believe, what Jesus' mission was all about. When Jesus described what was to happen in the days ahead, Peter tried to talk Him out of it. We know the response he received: "Get thee behind me Satan!" Sounds like a very harsh volley from Jesus to Peter? Very much so. But Jesus knew what was in Peter's heart, He knew those weren't exactly Peter's words, but the one who was bent on stopping the actions. While the humanity in Peter came out, Jesus spoke to the spiritual side that wasn't Peter.

I imagine Peter's worst human moment (recorded anyway) was his denial of Jesus after the trial. This is the one Jesus predicted. Peter could never imagine an instance where he would deny being a follower of Jesus. In this case, Peter denied even knowing Him. Sometimes I struggle with these events. What was the desired lesson here? I still have trouble discerning that. But I do know that Jesus did not turn His back on Peter, in any of these instances. Even with Peter's lack of conviction in his belief, Jesus never left Peter. What does Peter's story tell us about belief?

There is another of the 12 professing belief in Jesus. This man walked alongside Jesus, with Peter and the rest of the gang. He saw the same things Jesus did. He heard the same things Jesus said. He ate, slept and traveled with Jesus, just like the rest of the 12. Yet his perspective of a "saving" Jesus was much different, and expected much different results. Judas' story is told in several varying lights. Some say he was a selfish tax collector that was only concerned with his own interests. Others say he was caught up in the many revolts of the day, a very impressionable person that would follow the crowd. Judas is an interesting study in "belief."

I think Judas did believe strongly in Jesus' mission. He followed Him just like the rest, giving up his livelihood the way the others did to learn more about Jesus. He bought into Jesus' prophecies, the way He carried Himself, and His teachings. I believe Judas shared the others' love for Jesus.

But just like Peter, the humanistic side of Judas was much too prevalent. Judas had his own ideas of what was salvation, just like Peter. Jesus, according to Judas, just needed the right stage…

Chapter Six
Favorite Disciple?

Then one of the Twelve – the one called Judas Iscariot – went to the chief priests and asked "What are you willing to give me if I hand him over to you?" So they counted out for him thirty silver coins. From then on Judas watched for an opportunity to hand him over.
Matthew 26:14-16

Judas Iscariot, keeper of the purse, follower of Jesus. He was one of the Twelve, giving up his livelihood to follow Jesus. He traveled with Jesus and the gang, listening and witnessing. He had the same experiences as the rest, even Peter. He knew there was something about this man called

Jesus. It is within these travels with Jesus that Judas began to contemplate the whole scenario. He heard Jesus talk about freedom for the oppressed, the weak, the ones under slaves rule. All men are created equal, no man shall stand taller than another. Jesus talked about a new Kingdom, a new order, and of course, the Messiah.

Judas new the Jews were waiting for such a man, such a moment in time. Being under Roman tyrannical rule was not an easy life. He saw the frustrations of the people as he collected their taxes. I imagine he was fairly well off, surely he didn't live the fishermen's life of the others. Some of the Twelve wondered why he was allowed to join the group. He was not a Galilean, like the others. Iscariot - "a man from Kerioth," in Judea. As one of Jesus' followers, he would have been considered one of the least likely to betray Jesus.

Much is written about Judas. John's Gospel account has Jesus referring to Judas as a devil (John 6:70-71.) My impression of Judas is different than some of these accounts, and is shared by many in the Biblical scholar roundtable.

Judas was an intelligent person, he held ranking in the Roman order as a tax collector. Yet he became intrigued by this man called Jesus, so much that he began to follow Him. In the Gospel accounts, Jesus picks the Twelve he would empower to become disciples. Interestingly enough, Judas is always listed as the last one picked, or at least the last one listed, and it follows in each case that Judas was the one who would betray Jesus. Judas was very taken by Jesus, and probably felt the power Jesus seemed to harness meant something very special to the Jews. Judas believed in Jesus, no doubt, but was Jesus' mission the thing Judas really believed in?

When conversations arise about who the greatest disciple is, does Judas get any votes? Peter usually wins out, but Judas believed in what he thought Jesus could do. Problem was, Jesus had other ideas about salvation, not just in the present time. Judas was looking for an earthly rule, one who could defeat the Romans and provide "freedom for the prisoners." This meant something different for Judas than it did for Jesus, of course. Judas was sure THIS was the man for whom the Jews waited, finally the Roman empire will meet its match. He was ready to fight alongside Jesus, for Jesus could lead these people out from slavery into lives filled with riches. Judas' humanity got in the way of his thinking, similar to Peter when Peter would try to keep Jesus from filling His mission. Clearly, the Twelve didn't realize the magnitude of Jesus' mission; they held close to their human ideals.

What gets overlooked in many critical studies of the Gospels is Judas' passion for Jesus. Of course Judas was a little skewed on the mission part, but he believed in Jesus, at least as passionately as Peter and the rest. When the time came for Peter to stand up and declare his involvement with Jesus, he denied knowing Him. Judas not only admitted knowing Him, he even led the officials from the chief priests and Pharisees to Him. Judas did not deny his involvement with Jesus, and was boastful about knowing Him. Who would be depicted as having more belief in Jesus? Judas led the soldiers to Jesus, Peter denied knowing Jesus altogether.

Although the mission held a very different meaning for Judas, he followed through with what he believed. Some scholars equate Judas' intentions as hopefully providing the spark that would spur Jesus to act. This action was to begin the battle for earthly supremacy, to overthrow the Romans and set the Jews free. Judas bought into this notion and felt Jesus was to be that leader. Judas grew tiresome of Jesus' unwillingness to confront the earthly battle. As we learned in Matthew, Judas began to look for the right time to push Jesus into position. At the Last Supper, which I am sure none of the Twelve realized the significance of, the time seemed better than ever. Jesus even sends Judas out from the feast; "What you are about to do, do quickly." John says "As soon as Judas took the bread, Satan entered into him" John 13:27. Doesn't this sound familiar?

"Get thee behind me Satan" were the words He spoke to Peter.

It is an eerie set of circumstances. Peter invokes his famous "you are the Christ" then imparts his own human mission into Jesus' mission, to which Jesus responds. In the same light, Judas, feeling Jesus needs a little help, imparts his own human mission into play, and Satan is called out as the instigator once again. Both men have a human streak that goes against Jesus' mission. Both men believe in their own feelings. Both men play a part in the Easter story.

Does one man believe more than the other? Is either man's belief in accord with Jesus' mission? Does what we believe hold the same things?

Studying the actions of Judas and Peter in accordance with Jesus is a good way to begin self study. In each of these cases, they felt committed to Jesus, but for gravely different reasons. They both held passions for their personal beliefs; but clearly did not hold tightly, or understand, Jesus and His mission. Judas always gets the bad rap; I am sure we all have friends named Peter, but how many friends do we know named Judas (or consequently any Pontius Pilates?). The results of their actions are undoubtedly related. Peter wept bitterly, Judas hanged himself. Both realized the fallibility of their own beliefs, and the true meaning of Jesus' mission.

Are we like the original Twelve, and Judas/Peter? Do we entwine our own beliefs into Jesus' mission? Are we ready to follow Jesus and His mission without determining how we can help?

Chapter Seven
Believe

From Merriam-Webster:

*Main Entry: **be·lieve,** Pronunciation: \bə-'lēv\, Function: verb, Inflected Form(s): **be·lieved; be·liev·ing,** Etymology: Middle English beleven, from Old English belēfan, from be-+ly'fan, lēfan to allow, believe; akin to Old High German gilouben to believe, Old English lēof dear - more at love, Date: before 12th century Intransitive Verb - **1a:** to have a firm religious faith, **b:** to accept as true, genuine, or real <ideals we believe in> <believes in ghosts> **2:** to have a firm conviction as to the goodness, efficacy, or ability of something <believe in <u>exercise</u>> **3:** to hold an opinion : <u>think</u> <I believe so>, Transitive Verb - **1a:** to consider to be true or honest <believe the reports> <you wouldn't believe how long it took> **b:** to accept the word or evidence of <I believe you> <couldn't believe my ears> **2:** to hold as an opinion : <u>suppose</u> <I believe it will rain soon>, **be·liev·er** noun, **not believe** : to be astounded at <I couldn't believe my luck>*

Believe is a strong word. Humans profess belief in a multitude of things. But what does "I believe" really mean?

In Mark, chapter 9 verses 14-29, Jesus heals a boy of an evil spirit. Jesus happens upon a crowd that is engaged in an argument with the teachers of the law. Jesus asks what are they arguing about? The father describes the problem - his son is possessed. He asked Jesus' disciples to drive out the demon, but they cannot. The father asks Jesus, "If you can do anything, take pity on us and help us."

"If you can?" says Jesus. "Everything is possible for him who believes."

Immediately the boy's father exclaimed, "I do believe; help me overcome my unbelief!"

I do believe. Help me overcome my unbelief. That is tough to wrestle with. I do believe, help me overcome my unbelief. Do we feel that way sometimes? Since faith is never perfect, belief and unbelief are often mixed. Does that make one an un-believer? I am sure at times it may represent just that. If you are like me, and most are I would gather, humanity causes us to question many things. How can Jesus take on our sins? How can God sacrifice Himself to make US right in His eyes?

More simply, how could I have hooked my seven-iron that far left, miss the green altogether and land in the water? (Sorry, it has been a while since a golf interjection. I have unbelief in those instances as well.)

I think I can illustrate an incidence of simultaneous belief and unbelief.

I was at Pine Valley in New Jersey taking some pictures for a project I was working on. Pine Valley is annually ranked as the top golf course in the world and is very majestic. My group started their day on the 10th tee and I was going to meet up with them back on the first tee after I finished taking video of some of the other holes. When I completed my video time, the group approached the first tee and one of the members asked me if I would like to play the front nine holes. Of course I did…

I hit my first tee shot down the middle, hit a beautiful 9 iron to the green and two putted for par. Same routine on the second hole. The group must not have played the back nine too well because the caddies we had were all excited. "We finally got a golfer," they exclaimed to each other. I continued on the par binge until I bogeyed the fifth, a storied par three that I missed the green from the tee into a sand bunker. Then I continued on my march, each hole building more confidence. I stood on the ninth tee a mere one over par; a birdie on 9 and I would attain legend status…even par for the day.

At this point I believed I could make birdie. I already had a couple good chances for birdie, but my putter wasn't cooperating. My caddy assured me we would find a way to make birdie, finish the nine holes at even par and then the celebration would begin. With this confidence instilled in me, I set the ball on the tee and began the assault…

My driver connected with the ball the way it had all day; solidly. The ball began its flight slightly right of my intended target but not in bad shape when all of a sudden it hit what golfer's refer to as the "plexi-glass wall in the sky." It went right. It kept going right. It didn't stop going right. It disappeared over the first several rows of trees in the woods. I didn't see or hear it land. The only sound I did hear was my caddy; "that is the worst tee shot I have ever seen," he tried to whisper to the other caddy...

My belief turned sharply to disbelief.

I had to tee another one because under the rules of golf, a lost ball penalizes you twice. You play a second ball from the same spot and it costs you a penalty shot, so you actually get a stroke and distance penalty. You really don't want to lose your ball.

Now the rules provide that you may hit a "provisional" when there is doubt about where your ball landed, allowing you to hit another shot but you may play the first ball if you find it. You must announce to the group your intention to put into play a provisional ball. (There is no "real" mulligan in golf, but I sure could have used one here.) I announced I was hitting a provisional. The other caddy let out a muffled laugh, highly impolitely I might add, and proclaimed "you must be kidding, that ball is on the beltway going south by now." Nice.

My "provisional" landed in a fairway sand bunker. There was no celebrated search for the first tee shot, it was gone. From there I would be hitting my fourth shot. Birdie was no longer an option at this point. Another bit of golf nuance; shooting a 39 for nine holes is a lot nicer than only one stroke better than shooting 40. It is like buying a car for $19,995 rather than paying $20,000. Huge difference. At this point, my goal was now to not surpass 39 for the round.

I had a couple strokes to give, in that I was still just 1 over par, 36 being even par for the nine holes. At one over, a par would net me 37. I could live with that however I would have to hole out the bunker shot. No real chance for that to happen, so I did not believe at this point par was even attainable. I believed I could get the ball on the green and perhaps even one putt - that would get me to 38, still a good round especially at Pine Valley. My ball headed out of the sand onto the green.

Pine Valley's greens are not easy to read. I had a caddy however. If I could get this putt close and make the next one, I would be at 39, salvaging the day and still attain some form of immortality. I believed…

My first putt (now you know this will require at least one more putt because of the use of "first,") eased past the hole and continued to roll. I believed it would stop. It did not. I was now left with a 6 foot putt back up the hill. Disbelief struck me momentarily. For those of you who have never played golf with me, putting is not my forte. But I had a caddy. He believed in me.

As we sized up the next putt into or out of immortality, I still believed. As my putt rolled toward the cup, I still believed. When the ball caught the edge of the hole and spun out, so did my belief. The ball rolled at least halfway back to me. I still had three feet to cover. And I just played my 39th shot of the round. The three-footer didn't go in either. I tapped in for

41. I covered the last hole in a mere 8 shots; the dreaded snowman, quadruple bogey.

My joyous belief at the tee box turned to solemn disbelief. Little did I know at the time I would have a story to share with you about belief and disbelief all wrapped up into one moment. I did not, however, have any problem reliving that sequence of events as the story got told an infinite number of times upon our arrival back in Texas. But not by me.

I do believe, help me overcome my disbelief. There you have it.

Belief in Jesus is often presented as a "pre-requisite" for "gaining" salvation through Him. People quote verses in the Bible that point to this. In our Creed we say every Sunday, we profess to believe in God the Father, God the Son, and God the Holy Spirit, belief in the triune God. But is belief a requirement for salvation?

Ephesians 2:8-9 – Paul writes to the saints in Ephesus:

"For it is by grace you have been saved, through faith - and this is not from yourselves, it is a gift from God - not by works, so that no one may boast."

Paul says our salvation is vetted by God's grace, not our works or deeds. This is relayed over and over in the New Testament. It is a staple in Martin Luther's reformation. We do not earn God's grace, it is bestowed upon us through the works of Jesus. In *Lutheran Basics,* it tells us –

"Grace is the love of God, embodied in Jesus Christ, that makes us holy and beloved people of God. The gospel, or the good news, tells us we do nothing to earn this love. It is

70

absolutely free, on the house, pure gift. 'The story of human sin is the story of our rebellion against God...We place ourselves first, before God.' In spite of this, God never abandons us. Rather, God embraces us with lavish generosity, conquering death on our behalf and offering us life. In every way, in everything we do, in all we are, God is for us. This is Grace."

Remember the couple I described at the outset of this book, the ones from Texas? Of course you do. They had a very simple phrase that I thought was absolutely genius. It was responsibility. Only she spelled it response-ability. We will tackle that one in a minute.

In Paul's letter to the Ephesians, he explains grace. We aren't mandated to accept or receive this grace. God gives this gift out of His love for us, regardless of our response, regardless of our actions. One recurring quote from the cross by Jesus - "Forgive them Father, for they know not what they do" Luke 23:34. I always wonder who Jesus meant by "they." Was it the people who put the nails in the cross? Was it the Crowd? Was it the Romans in general?

Or perhaps, humanity itself?

Chapter Eight
"Father, Forgive Them..."

On the cross that day, Jesus did a lot of things, didn't he? What a day.

We have the situation of who was crucified with Him. Two criminals. They belonged on the cross that day. They broke the rules. Pilate was making examples of them. That was the ultimate goal of crucifixion; to make an example of what lies ahead for you if you cross the Roman rule. Besides being a tortuous way to die, it was a very public spectacle. Humanity have always been news watchers. We can't look away when something like this happens. We become glued to the action. Hanging someone wasn't enough, they don't suffer very long. Crucifixion was far more effective in deterring crime. The two criminals crucified that day along with Jesus deserved their fate.

Luke 23:39-43:

"One of the criminals who hung there hurled insults as him: 'Aren't you the Christ? Save yourself and us!' But the other criminal rebuked him. 'Don't you fear God,' he said, 'since you are under the same sentence? We are punished justly, for we are getting what our deeds deserve. But this man has done nothing wrong.' Then he said 'Jesus, remember me when you come into your kingdom.' Jesus answered him, 'I tell you the truth, today you will be with me in paradise.'"

Here we have another interesting comparison in the discussion about belief. One criminal mocks Jesus as they hang on the cross. "Save us and yourself!" I wonder what would have happened had Jesus done that? But the other criminal rebukes him. His belief is strong - "Jesus remember me when you come into your kingdom." As he hangs on the cross, he asks Jesus to remember him. Of course Jesus knows that "today you will be with me in paradise."

Did both criminals make it to paradise that day?

"Father forgive them, for they know not what they do."

This is Jesus' only real answer to those who persecuted Him that day. He bore the sins of humanity, took up the penalty for sin and made it His own. He conquered death with His rising again, and with that act He claimed death for all sinners, giving new life; rebirth. He told this to Nicodemus on that night they talked. To enter the Kingdom of heaven, you must be born again. Humanity was not worthy of the gifts God gives. Humanity must be reborn, renewed, made righteous. What is impossible for man is possible with God.

Notice Jesus doesn't say "Father forgive them, for they believe in Me," or "Father forgive them as they have repented." No, Jesus asks for the mercy of God to take over. They know not what they do. Jesus' actions on the cross give compelling answers to a host of questions, as does His words and actions before the cross.

As I discussed earlier, belief is somewhat of a mystery. Do we believe, how much do we believe, how we believe - is relative to our personal environment. Can we believe and still have doubt? What makes a true believer? Does belief, or non-belief, change the validity of things? The outcome of something? Have an effect on the actions of others?

God reconciles man (humanity) to Himself by His own action. What is impossible for man is possible through God. Does God need our assistance? Do we show love for God to "get" His Grace? Does God give grace because we ask, earn, deserve it?

Let's go back to the couple in Texas. Remember the term response-ability? Literally this is the "ability to respond." Responsibility. Do we have a "responsibility" to God, or is it more of a "response-ability" from God? Paul says even our faith is a gift from God. FROM God. Our own faith and "belief" *in* God comes *from* God. In Romans 3:3-4, Paul asks the curious question; "what if some did not have faith? Will their lack of faith nullify God's faithfulness? Not at all! Let God be true, and every man a liar..." I will let you read the rest for yourself.

So our belief does not cause God to act. He acts on His own accord. He isn't responding to humanity's request.

The Third chapter in Romans discusses plenty on the topic of "who is God's grace for." Romans, as we learned earlier, was the basis for Martin Luther's Reformation, for he learned that God's Grace does not come through any human action - rather from God Himself. A study of Romans reveals the whole issue on Grace, 3:20 tells us "Therefore no one will be declared righteous in his sight by observing the law; rather through the law we become conscious of sin."

If believing in God means to follow the laws handed down, this alone would not provide our salvation, for a couple reasons. First, as humans we cannot follow the law, we are Sin. We prove that every day in our humanistic actions. Jesus came, as He told Nicodemus, because humans cannot follow the law, God's Law. Second, as we see in this and other places in the Bible, even with Jesus' own words, the Law was not given for us to follow; rather is it a means to show what Sin is, what our sinful nature is, what our transgressions are.

So - in "believing," we cannot simply live a life according to God's Law, by God's own admission (Jesus). However - in 3:23, Paul says- "for all have sinned and fall short of the glory of God, (24) and are justified freely by his grace through the redemption that came by Christ Jesus. (25) God presented him as a sacrifice of atonement, through faith in his blood. He did this to demonstrate his justice, because in his forbearance he left the sins committed beforehand unpunished - (26) he did it to demonstrate his justice at the present time, so as to be just and the one who justifies those who have faith in Jesus."

Chapter 5 in Romans speaks more to Grace imparted through the actions of Jesus. Again this is where Luther received his illumination. I would invite you to read Romans Chapter 5, again if you already have!

Belief in God, Jesus' mission, grace - does it have any eternal effect? We know that God sent Jesus to do what He did. God wasn't gambling that Jesus *might* be rejected. He knew what the score was. He knew what lied ahead for Jesus, and of course so did Jesus. He attempted to explain this to His disciples. We know Peter's response - "Jesus, don't go to Jerusalem, save yourself." It is part of God's plan - indeed it is His plan - for redeeming mankind through the actions of Jesus, and what was to happen to Jesus on earth. He knows of humanity's unbelief, yet still He acts.

This action was not in response to anything but His own will. It wasn't dependent on any actions by humanity. Certainly humanity wasn't deserving of any grace.

People are funny when it comes to "who gets God's grace," aren't they? It is often interesting, although frustrating, to converse with those who feel they are more worthy of God's grace - mostly because of how they perceive their own actions and faithfulness. It is also interesting to see whom they feel won't receive God's grace. Paul addresses this as well in his commentary that is Romans.

Romans Chapter 14 is a curious study regarding these issues. As the Church, in present day, struggles with many issues, including homosexuality, which is a major topic for division in the Lutheran church today, Paul offers a wonderful view. It speaks to belief and what effect different beliefs have. I will save you the effort of getting out of your comfortable setting and transcribe the Chapter here.

"Accept him whose faith is weak, without passing judgment on disputable matters. One man's faith allows him to eat everything, but another man, whose faith is weak, eats only vegetables. The man who eats everything must not look down on him who does not, and the man who does not eat everything must not condemn the man who does, for God has accepted him. Who are you to judge someone else's servant? To his own master he stands or falls. And he will stand, for the Lord is able to make him stand.

One man considers one day more sacred than another; another man considers every day alike. Each one should be fully convinced in his own mind. He who regards one day as special, does so to the Lord. He who eats meat, eats to the Lord, for he gives thanks to God; and he who abstains, does so to the Lord and gives thanks to God. For none of us lives to himself alone, and none of us dies to himself alone. If we live, we live to the Lord;

and if we die, we die to the Lord. So, whether we live or die, we belong to the Lord.

For this very reason, Christ died and returned to life so the He might be the Lord of both the dead and the living. You, then, why do you judge your brother? Or why do you look down on your brother? For we all stand before God's judgment seat. It is written: 'As surely as I live, says the Lord, every knee will bow before me; every tongue will confess to God.'

So then each of us will give an account of himself to God.

Therefore let us stop passing judgment on one another. Instead, make up your mind not to put any stumbling block or obstacle in your brother's way. As one who is in the Lord Jesus, I am fully convinced that no food is unclean in itself. But if any one regards something as unclean, then for him it is unclean. If your brother is distressed because of what you eat, you are no longer acting in love. Do not by your eating destroy your brother for whom Christ died. Do not allow what you consider good to be spoken of as evil. For the kingdom of God is not a matter of eating and drinking, but of righteousness, peace and joy in the Holy Spirit, because *anyone who serves Christ in this way is pleasing to God and approved by men.*

Let us therefore make every effort to do what leads to peace and to mutual edification. Do not destroy the work of God for the sake of food. All food is clean, but it is wrong for a man to eat anything that causes someone else to stumble. It is better not to eat meat or drink wine or to do anything else that will cause your brother to fall.

So whatever you believe about these things keep between yourself and God. Blessed is the man who does not condemn himself by what he approves. But the man who has doubts is condemned if he eats, because his eating is not from faith; and everything that does not come from faith is sin."

Romans 14

His is an interesting essay to say the least. It deals with those who differ on what "believing" means. If one believes a certain thing - and another believes differently, who determines the correct belief? Paul's essay says it doesn't matter, as neither of the two gets to judge anyway. Whether we "believe" one way, or "believe" in another way, those differences do not make for judgment opportunities. We should rejoice in "belief" regardless. Paul's words speak of making "rules" for us to live by, believe by, and how irrelevant those rules are. God makes us His - we don't justify ourselves to God by living according to our rules, or even His rules. For that way of life is no way of life. We will never be able to fulfill the life of living up to the rules.

But Paul says we can cause brothers to stumble, create obstacles, by challenging the beliefs of others; by comparing those beliefs to our own in an attempt to be more "righteous." Paul says, in Chapter 15:7 – "Accept one another, then, just as Christ accepted you, in order to bring praise to God." Paul is saying that we don't all have to come to the same conclusion on matters of conscience, but that we might agree to disagree in Christian love.

So even in "believing" – there doesn't have to be a consensus. This goes back to the wonderful assessment of Pastor Fred Toerne; The infinite number of ways there are to Christ. Each in his own way - God's Grace is sufficient. There is no "correct" way to believe- no recipe, no standard. There can be no human judgment of one another's belief. In the end (and of course the beginning - and all in between) we are God's - and not by our own actions or by our own belief; but by the work of God Himself.

So what if no one believed?

Chapter Nine

Disciples 2

What if no one believed?

An interesting study in belief is offered through the lives of the disciples. We discussed Peter and Judas; very different belief systems there, but as we also portrayed - similar in that they were interested in having Jesus act in accordance with their own understanding of Jesus' mission. Or at least their human sides became revealed - with the assistance of Satan anyway...

God works out a plan, doesn't He? He gathers 12 men to follow Him, giving them the opportunity to live with Jesus for a few years; hearing His words, watching His actions, allowing the questions to be asked, and even asking them a few things from time to time. What a cast He assembles.

One of my favorite passages in the Bible comes from

Matthew Chapter 4:18-22. Here Jesus tells Simon (called Peter) and his brother Andrew – "Come, follow me and I will make you fishers of men." I am sure we can all relate to someone in our lives who can illustrate a "fisher of men." A lot of times we equate this with a Pastor - their words from God cause us to come to church each Sunday and listen. Relationships get formed because of the common bond we share, namely inclusion in the Body of Christ.

My Great Uncle Ralph Swanson passed away recently. He was my father's mother's brother; that would make him my father's uncle, translating to mean he was my great uncle. As my brother Doug would say at Uncle Ralph's funeral; he was our Great Uncle, but he was also a great brother, a great father, a great husband and a great friend. Uncle Ralph (many in our family referred to him simply as "Unc") had Christ's love in his heart, as we all do, but Uncle Ralph (I did not refer to him as Unc) lived a life that flowed from the love Christ first gives us. When someone shows that love, Christ's Love, and lives in the spirit of that love, people can see this. Uncle Ralph made no doubt about the love that was in his heart, it came from Jesus. He was a wonderful example of what it means to live a life that is free in God's Love. My father Gary has the same qualities; I am sure as an extension and example of the life Uncle Ralph lived. Uncle Ralph's life, and lifestyle, affected many people and is the living paradigm for what it means to be a "fisher of men." Simply by his actions, inspired by Christ's Love within him, he brought that love to others.

The disciples were given a greater opportunity; the chance to see the Love of Christ first hand. They witnessed many things, the Gospels even say they witnessed many things not even recorded in these pages. They followed Jesus, forming their own opinions about what they saw and heard. I am sure many times they were unsure of what was happening - and perhaps even frightful of the potential consequences they could face because of the words and actions Jesus presented. But they listened, heard, saw, witnessed, and even quarreled.

Matthew 4:21-22 tells us that James and John were in a boat with their father Zebedee. When "Jesus called them, they immediately left the boat - and their father - and followed Him." That is pretty powerful stuff. They left their father. But they also left their way of life, their family, their environment, everything. They were stripped bare of the earthly things they were accustomed to. They believed in Jesus enough to do this. Perhaps it was a higher calling that compelled them to follow...

I find it fascinating following the journey these men embarked on. Jesus brings them along - telling them things they never heard, showing them things they never saw before. Questioning them, and even answering their questions from time to time. Dealing with their misgivings about His mission constantly. James and John came to Jesus, as told in Mark 10:35-45 (also you can see Matthew 20:20-28.) In Mark's account, the brothers ask if they can sit on Jesus' right and left hand in His kingdom (in Matthew, it is their mother's request.) Jesus tells them to become great, they must become servants; to be first they must be last; that just like the Son of Man did not come to be served, but to serve, and to give his life as a ransom for many. I think they struggled with these kinds of words from Jesus. But yet they continued to follow Him.

They often struggled with healing. In one instance, they attempt to stop someone from healing because he does not embark the action in the name of Jesus. Jesus rebukes them in this instance, saying whomever is not against you is with you...I imagine this was confusing as well. The disciples question Jesus quite a bit, and even in some of the answers to Jesus questions they show confusion, or at least a less-than-full understanding of His mission. They see the multiple times people try to "trap" Jesus with their circumstantial questions, and see Jesus use His words to answer their queries.

Of course we discussed Peter and his bouts with belief - or at least not understanding the mission. Thomas shows his humanity with a call to witness the wounds in Jesus' body. Judas epitomizes human thinking by attempting to prod Jesus into performing what Judas feels is the right thing to do. Throughout Jesus' ministry, He deals with all kinds of belief, disbelief, misunderstanding, confusion, contempt, loyalty, discussion...the realms of humanity coming from His chosen disciples.

But discipleship wasn't free, according to Jesus. He tells this in several passages throughout the NT. In many of these conversations, Jesus knows just what to "require" when someone asks if he can follow Him. One man is about to bury his father - Jesus tells him "let the dead bury the dead." Another man asks, and Jesus tells him to give all his riches to the poor, then he can truly follow Him. He tells a gathering of people in Luke 14:25-27:

"Large crowds were traveling with Jesus, and turning to them He said: 'If anyone comes to me and does not hate his father and mother, his wife and children, his brothers and sisters - yes, even his own life - he cannot be my disciple. And anyone who does not carry his cross and follow me cannot be my disciple.'"

That's pretty lofty stuff.

I was aware of this passage, but became intimately united with it when a pastor in Houston was leaving for vacation and asked me if I would be willing to give a message at the Sunday service. I said sure, of course. I asked what shall I talk about and he told me to read the lessons for the day and talk about the Gospel. Sounds easy enough.

Then I read the Gospel. Luke 14:25-35. Nice. I still have trouble forgiving him.

But it caused me to study what this passage is saying. It also caused me to look at what else Jesus has to say about the "cost" of being a disciple. It seems to me, like I said earlier, Jesus has a way of asking people to look inside, and give up the things that may be the most important to them, as a way of showing He is looking for complete surrender to Him. For some, the hardest material item to give up is money.

"Go and sell all you have, and give that money to the poor." The man turned away, unable to do as Jesus directs. In another instance in Luke, someone says, "I will follow you, Lord; but first let me go back and say goodbye to my family." Jesus responds, "No one who puts his hand to the plow and looks back is fit for service in the kingdom of God."

The people who do not follow - unbelievers? Are those who follow "better" believers?

If we take Jesus at his word, it seems like an easy question to answer. But I believe these passages have a much deeper meaning than just the surface words. Jesus speaks to each of us in, His way, voices that are understood by the hearer. Remember the words of Pastor Fred Toerne - many different ways Jesus comes to each of us. What may be easy for someone to give up is impossible for someone else to even consider. Does that make one a better follower of Jesus? Believe stronger? Does this make a difference in the end? Does the strength of one's belief, or any belief at all, have an impact?

Chapter Ten
The Journey

"Then Jesus told him, 'Because you have seen me, you have believed; blessed are those who have not seen and yet have believed.'"

John 20:29

Jesus tells this to "Believing Thomas," as Pastor Fred calls him.

At the end of this theological journey that is "What If No One Believed" we see many variables, conversations, consequences, discussion, theological interpretation - but conclusions? Harder to come by.

Mark's account has the disciples displaying unbelief after the Resurrection - first Mary's account, then the two men who met Jesus as they were walking in the country. Mark says Jesus rebuked them for their lack of faith and their stubborn refusal to believe those who saw Him after he had risen. Then of course, He sends them out to evangelize.

The Gospels report that Jesus breathed on them - and they were covered with the Holy Spirit - and their eyes were opened. Their minds were opened. They saw - but more importantly they understood. Only when God intercedes do their minds open - and they are ready to receive what Jesus is telling them.

"What is impossible for man - is possible for God."

The Good News of the New Testament is; "Jesus Saves!" No act of man changes that. No act of man warrants that. This is God's doing, at God's direction. God's Riches At Christ's Expense. GRACE. It is really that simple. And – it is the ONLY way it can happen. Paul says the act of one man's disobedience causes humanity to become Sin - the act of one man's sacrifice causes man to become reconciled. Martin Luther read Romans and the Reformation began. Man does not pay for his own salvation, the cost is too great. But - what is impossible for man is possible with God.

Rebirth - Jesus tells Nicodemus it is impossible for a man to enter the kingdom unless he is reborn - born again - made new. He wasn't describing the physical birth of the individual here. Jesus was describing His mission; the renewal of humanity in its relationship with God, a mission only God can complete. Reconciliation between God and humanity. We do nothing because there is nothing we can do.

It is ironic that humanity's disbelief in Jesus played a huge role in the Easter scenario. The Rabbis, Sadducees, religious leaders of the time, and most of the people living then did not believe Jesus, so they killed Him. The religious leaders knew of the Old Testament teachings, they knew the history, they knew eventually the Messiah was coming - why didn't they believe? Was it humanistic judgment? Did they like the way things were, not wanting to change their positions in society? Afraid of becoming something less than the heralded people they were? Jesus preached giving of one's self - above your own needs. The leaders back then didn't like that message at all. Jesus said He came to free the prisoners - with a message that man cannot do this - but possible with God. The Leaders preached methods of atonement to pay for one's sins, somehow man could gain favor with God through his own actions, living the godly life and of course, through monetary donations. It is precisely because of man's actions that humanity became Sin in the first place. Man needs a rebirth, a new start - a mulligan. Except - not only did God re-tee our ball, but He removes us from the tee box and inserts Jesus.

Jesus and Moses were playing golf one day, and they reached the par 5. Both hit good drives, Jesus hits His a little farther than Moses. So, Moses hits first. Now on this hole there is a large pond in front of the green, one that is not easily played over. Moses pulled out his iron and lays up a good shot in front of the pond - a safe play.

Upon approaching His ball, Jesus is contemplating His

position. He turns to Moses and asks, "What would Arnold Palmer do?" Moses replies that Arnie would pull his 3 wood out and challenge the pond, trying to reach the green in two shots. Hey, what's good enough for Arnold Palmer the King...

Jesus hits a ball that splashes into the pond.

Moses plays his third shot onto the green and continues to walk around the pond. Jesus calls to Moses, saying He is going to get His ball out of the pond - so he heads out - walking over the water.

Now the group on the next tee is watching the activity. As Moses approaches the green, a man asks, "What gives? Does your partner think he's Jesus Christ or something?"

Moses says, "No - He thinks He's Arnold Palmer."

Sometimes humanity gets it reversed. We think we need to make some grandstand play to gain salvation. We can do good - we can live according to the Law (or at least try real hard). We can atone for our sinful nature. Many people live their lives in an attempt to do just this. We give offerings to atone for certain behaviors or activities we do.

But in these "beliefs" we are like Peter and Judas. We know the story - we know what Jesus did for us, but still we try to help. In our attempt to "believe" we infuse our actions into the "act of the one who brought righteousness." For some, the gift isn't quite enough. Just as Jesus told Peter what must happen to Him, and Peter tries to infuse humanistic thinking into the equation, humanity often gets caught up in the event.

This kind of rational actually depicts a disbelief in God's

reconciliation. Many religious leaders of the present time promote the ideal of humanity's need to play a role in its "own reconciliation with God." They teach adherence to God's Laws as the yardage marker to salvation. Or they preach about redemption having to do with believing as a pre-requisite. Repent, be sorry, live a godly life, trust in Jesus. But Jesus tells us we can't. For if we repent, be sorry, live a godly life - (again, or try to) under the guise that if we just... try...real...hard - we can be saved, then the last part of the previous sentence goes away; Trust in Jesus. At this point, we don't trust in Jesus, we trust in our own (apparent) ability to please (?) God. Jesus' actions aren't enough alone to do the trick. We must act for ourselves. We must "accept" the gift of salvation in order to receive it.

But the reconciliation is not "humanity to God" – it is "from God to humanity."

It is funny how in humanity's attempt to "gain" salvation, we actually mirror the sinful nature that is our being. We start to measure how we are doing, comparing our attempts to others. Keep score. I am doing better than the next guy. I am not as bad as the next guy. We draw lines in the sand - what are "acceptable" actions and what are those that don't make the grade. We preach what is God's will for us, and condemn those that don't follow our own self-righteousness. We fight, argue and divide ourselves because of how words in the Bible are translated. We pick passages that support our own slant.

Jesus tells the adulterous woman, "...nor do I condemn

you. Go and live in sin no more."

Go and live in sin no more BECAUSE I do not condemn you. Jesus doesn't say, "Look, try a little harder, I will give you one more chance." Or "tell Me you are sorry, pay Me a sum of money, spend two years in jail, then I will forgive you and I will let you go." Or even, "Do you believe in Me? Then go and be free."

Jesus doesn't give us the keys to death, so we can unlock the door if we choose, by our own actions. Jesus defeated death, the payment for our sinful nature, and humanity rose from this depth on the Third Day, along with Jesus, to be reconciled with God. That is our rebirth - our cleansing, our renewal; impossible for man, possible with God. Just as humanity dies with Christ, humanity is reborn in the Resurrection.

Jesus does give us the keys to life. He gives us the response-ability. Without the worry and burden of our own sinful nature causing the separation from God, we live our lives free from that bondage. The chains are off. There is no need to keep score. There is no need to condemn the actions of others so we can look better. When God looks upon humanity, He sees Jesus, not Adam. Jesus represents humanity to God, in place of Adam. The condemnation of humanity through Adam becomes the redemption of humanity through Jesus.

Our belief, then, becomes the key to life in response to God's reconciliation of man; not a measure of our salvation. The salvation is ours, because of the action through Jesus.

Our belief in that doesn't change that. Our belief changes our own actions - or reactions, not God's.

Imagine a world that hinges on whether we are "good enough." You need to measure up or suffer eternal death. But no one knows exactly where the line is - who gets in, who doesn't. What acts are justifiable, what acts are horrific. Who gets to sip margaritas and who needs a fan for the afterlife. This is a world where no one believes; a world where we do whatever is necessary to insure we "look better" in comparison to the next guy. Sadly for some people, this is the reality in which they live. They may even profess to believe in Jesus, but do they really? If they did, they would be free from trying to gain salvation...

Amy Grant sings a song that describes what happens - believing that Jesus has already accomplished our salvation. A line from it says "We will be like Him, for we will see Him as He is.

"No longer what we were before, but not all that we will be; Tomorrow when we lock the door, on all our compromising; And He appears, He'll draw us near and we'll be changed by His Glory, Wrapped up in His Glory.

"We will be like Him, for we shall see Him as He is.

"No longer what we saw before, but not all that we will see; Tomorrow when we lock the door on all our disbelieving; When He appears, our view will clear and we'll be changed by His Glory, wrapped up in His Glory."

This is what happens when we DO believe - and effects our lives here on earth.

Through the actions of Jesus, we are ALREADY claimed in God's redemption. In Baptism, we affirm what God has done. Our Baptism reminds us of those actions. We are claimed as a child of God, sealed with His love. Cleansed by the water and purified through the Holy Spirit. A reminder of the power of the Resurrection.

We renew this cleansing every day. We return to our waters of Baptism every day, remembering that we are first chosen by God - through the Resurrection - our actions of the day won't change that. Our belief (or disbelief) won't change that. But in our belief in Jesus and His Mission, we have the "ability to respond" to the Salvific actions of the Resurrection. This is what Jesus calls us to do...

With our eternal lives safely packed away we are free to live the life Jesus teaches us to. He gives us new commandments - "Love thy neighbor as thyself," "Forgive your brother- seventy times seven," "Feed my sheep," and finally - "Come, follow me and I will make you...Fishers of Men."

In Lewis Groce's book, *Fear Not!* he gives a wonderful story about his mother and Baptism...If you haven't read his book, you should. The return to our Baptism, daily, is a concept heavily promoted by the good Reverend Lewis. Daily Baptismal renewal allows us to begin each day equipped with the knowledge that we are God's children, reconciled with Him, by Him. When we take this knowledge to heart - believe - our lives do change. The embodiment of Jesus' love for us gets projected outwardly from us, and we can live

Christ-centered lives.

I like to project the effects of Christ's love in this illustration - follow along;

Imagine camp ground on the side of a wooded hill. On the other side of the ravine is another wooded hill. Across the ravine you can see a small clearing where a campfire is burning - the night is clear and you can't begin to count the stars in the sky. The fire is a small one but you can make out the flames as they shoot upward.

The flame dances on the face of the one who sits at the fire, and the reflection seems to glow from him. Soon others join around the fire. The light seems to grow as more people gather around, pulled in by the light and the warmth. All the while, the flames cast their reflection outward off the people who come in contact with it - and the small fire becomes larger in that reflection. Soon you are able to see the campfire from even farther away - this causes more people to join in the captivating light.

This is how Christ's love works. The glow of His love is in every man. When we get drawn near to His flame, the reflection bounces off outwardly, catching the attention of those around us. In turn, those affected by that glow reflect it onward to others. The flame doesn't change, it is the effect it has on us that causes it to grow. Our lives get transformed as we come in contact with the flame that is in each of us.

Our "believing" changes OUR lives, not God's actions. Without belief - the flame doesn't "grow." It stays lit on some hillside where no one can see it. But as we are drawn to the fire - believing in the flame - the warmth and illumination of God's love for humanity is multiplied, casting its life-giving qualities to, and from, each and every reflection.

Do we stand across the ravine, looking at the fire from far away, wondering what it would be like to be close to flame?

"Come, follow me..."

About The Author

David D. Edsall was born in Jamestown, New York, and moved to Maryland when he was 13 years old. His travels took him to Texas, where he lived for 10 years prior to moving back to Maryland.

Growing up, he was instilled with a strong faith by his parents, Martha and Gary, Sr., along with his two brothers, Douglas and Gary, Jr. The ideals and beliefs held by his family of Betteses, Swansons and Edsalls propelled his faith journey. David's beliefs have been tested and proven strong through serving as the President of several Church Councils, in Maryland and Texas.

His spiritual growth continues as he stays active in the church. Especially noted is his friendship with Pastor Lewis Groce, author of *Fear Not! A Layman's Guide to Theology*. Rev. Groce and David became partners in Edsall Golf Group, a Texas partnership, and their faith journey continues today. Dr. Ken Holder, a biblical scholar in his own right, remains connected in a very close friendship. Throughout his life, Dave has encountered many pastors, theologians and friends that have helped shape his perspective. These continued contacts offer further illumination to the mystery of God's Grace - a journey that is life itself.

David's use of golf insets draws from his experience as a Golf Course Architect. He is the Principal in Dave Edsall Golf Design, Inc., based in Maryland. Dave's world class golf designs are spread throughout the US and abroad, and can be viewed at www.degolfdesign.com.

Made in the USA
Charleston, SC
19 May 2010